CARD TRICKS

Also by Geoffrey Lamb

Mental Magic Tricks
Secret Writing Tricks
Table Tricks

CARD TRICKS

by GEOFFREY LAMB

THOMAS NELSON INC., PUBLISHERS
Nashville / New York

Fourth Printing

Library of Congress Cataloging in Publication Data

Lamb, Geoffrey Frederick.
  Card tricks.

  SUMMARY: Explains step-by-step the execution of a variety of card tricks emphasizing the subtle art of "misdirection."
  English ed. published under title: Your book of card tricks.
  1. Card tricks—Juvenile literature. [1. Card tricks]
GV1549.L35   1973   795.4′38   72-13357
ISBN 0-8407-6300-X

CONTENTS

CARD TRICKS

A FEW WORDS OF ADVICE

Card tricks can be fun. But remember that their purpose is to entertain people. You must be careful to present them in the right way. What matters is *the effect on the spectators* of what you do. The method by which you achieve the effect is far less important than the effect itself.

Not one of the tricks in this book requires you to carry out tricky moves with your fingers. This does not mean, however, that you can present them without thought or practice. Since you do not have to bother about deceiving people by the dexterity of your fingers, you can give your full attention to misleading their minds.

This misleading of the spectators' minds is the basis of all good conjuring. Magicians usually call it *misdirection*. Don't be misled by the word into thinking that it means you have to distract the spectators' attention by gesticulating wildly with one hand while you do something tricky with the other. Misdirection is much more subtle than this. Very briefly, it consists of leading the spectators to give their main attention to something that is of no importance to the real secret of the trick.

A very obvious example will be found in the fourth trick in this book, which is performed by a simple mathematical calculation. The performer gives the impression, without laboring the point, that magnetism somehow enters into it, and I have known spectactors to hunt vainly for the pin that they believe must be hidden somewhere among the cards. You will find many other examples of misdirection in this book.

Don't be *too* eager to show people your tricks. Let your performance be something that they can look forward to.

Don't show too many tricks at one time. Four or five may be quite enough. It is far better to leave your audience wanting to see another trick than for your audience to leave before you have finished.

Aim at variety. For example, don't perform a whole string of tricks, all of which result in the disclosure of a card chosen by a member of the audience. If you examine the first five tricks in this book, for instance, you will find that they all have a slightly different theme. In the first, a selected card is found by the queen of hearts. The second trick is concerned with the counting of pips on three cards. The third deals with whether the cards in certain packets are odd or even in number. In the fourth trick the number of cards moved by a spectator is mysteriously revealed by the conjurer. In the fifth, a card appears to jump from one half of the pack to the other.

Never present a trick, however simple it seems, until you have gone through it several times in private. To present a trick properly you need to know exactly what to do and exactly what to say, and this can be achieved only by practice.

Finally, never show the audience how a trick is done, unless it is a very simple trick indeed. Not only will they think the less of you once they know the secret, but you will deprive yourself of the opportunity of performing the same trick again at a later date.

NOTE. Have a pack of cards handy when you read this book. You will find the instructions much easier to understand if you actually carry them out as you study them.

TERMS USED IN THIS BOOK

Audience. For convenience the term is used for any group of people to whom you are showing some tricks, even though the group may be just two or three friends. The term "spectator" is used for any individual member of the group.

Court cards. The picture cards—king, queen, jack.

Cut the pack. Lift off the upper half of the pack and place it beside the lower half. To "complete the cut," place this lower half on top of what was formerly the upper half.

Face down. With the back of the card showing.

Face up. With the number or picture showing.

Index. The figure or letter on the left-hand top corner (and, upside down, right-hand bottom corner) of each card.

Numbered cards. Those cards which are neither court cards nor jokers. The ace is included among the numbered cards and counts one. The numbered cards are sometimes referred to as "ordinary" cards.

Riffle. A movement with the cards suggesting that you have performed something magical, though in fact it has no real effect and requires no skill. Press your left fingers against the top of the pack, and run your right fingers sharply upward against one end of the cards, thus causing a flicking noise.

Do you know that the queen of hearts is able to read people's thoughts?

You can test her ability quite easily. Pick out the queen, together with twenty-nine other cards. Put two ordinary cards and the queen in a row, face upward, with the queen on the right.

Now ask a spectator to deal the remaining twenty-seven cards face downward into three heaps or piles, putting one card at a time on each pile in turn. The heaps should be placed a little below the three face-up cards. (Fig. 1.)

Get the spectator to look at the queen's pile and mentally choose any card in it. He must not show which one he has chosen, but he must remember which one it is.

Collect the heaps, leaving them face downward.

"We'd better give her one or two trials first," you remark. "She may be out of practice."

You deal out the cards again in three piles, giving one card at a time to each pile. Ask the spectator to see if his chosen card is in the queen's heap. If it is, you congratulate her on her skill. If it is not, you pick up

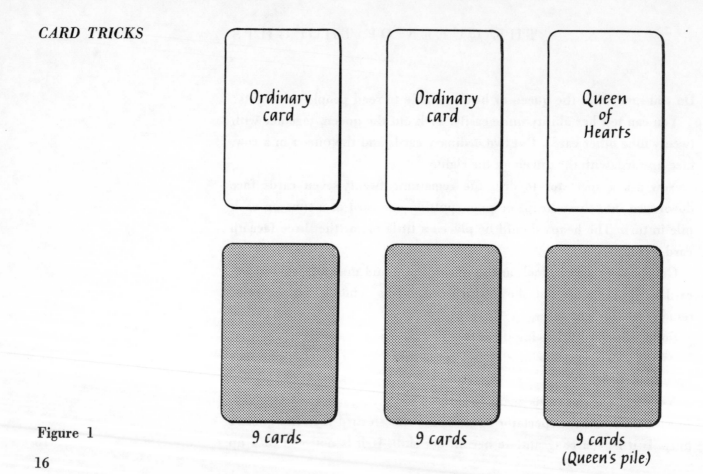

Figure 1

16

the pile containing the chosen card, fan the cards, and show them to the queen.

"I don't think she's really concentrating. We'd better give her another chance."

Whether the queen has succeeded or not, you gather up the three piles and deal out the cards once more. Again you ask if the chosen card is in the queen's pile.

If it is, you remark that she's obviously ready to do the trick. If it is not, you again show the pile containing the chosen card to the queen.

"She's had two trial runs," you comment. "Now she must try to do the trick on her own."

Once more you gather up the cards and deal them into three piles. This time, however, you do not ask the spectator to see which pile his card is in. You merely put aside the two piles on the left and take up the cards nearest to the queen.

"This is the pile she chooses. Let's hope she's right."

You deal the nine cards into three piles as before, but of course there are now only three cards in each pile.

Again you discard the two piles on the left and take up the pile the queen has "chosen." You deal out these three cards in order, the queen receiving the last one.

Pushing aside the two cards on the left, you ask the name of the chosen card. Then you turn over the queen's card. It is the very card that was mentally selected. The queen has successfully read the spectator's thoughts!

How it is done

All you have to do is to make sure that the pile containing the chosen card is at the bottom each time you gather up the three heaps. The queen then does the trick on her own. The selection of the card is automatic.

Points to remember

1. The first deal is carried out by the spectator. After this you collect and deal out the twenty-seven cards *three times*. The fourth time you deal only nine cards, and lastly only three cards.

2. Don't make it too obvious that the pile containing the chosen card is at the bottom each time you collect the cards. Just gather up the three heaps in a casual way. It does not matter which of the other two heaps is on top.

3. Don't draw attention to the fact that there are nine cards in each pile. Leave the spectators to find this out for themselves if they are sufficiently observant.

First of all remove the aces, kings, queens, and jokers. Then invite a spectator to act as your assistant. Ask him to shuffle the cards and deal out three cards face downward in a row.

"Nobody at present knows what cards they are," you point out. "But when I turn my back, I want you to put them face upward. Look at the index number of the first card. Then place enough cards on it, face downward, to bring the number up to fifteen. For instance, if the index number is two, you will require thirteen cards to make up fifteen. If the index number is five, you will require ten cards, if it's nine, you will require six cards, and so on. The jack, by the way, counts as a ten and needs five cards to bring it to fifteen.

"When you've done this with the first card, do the same thing with the other two cards."

You turn your back while your assistant carries out your instructions.

"Make sure that the face-up cards are completely covered, so that I can't see what they are," you tell him. "I'm going to add them up by magic. And I'll give you the result by picking out some cards that will add up to exactly the same as yours."

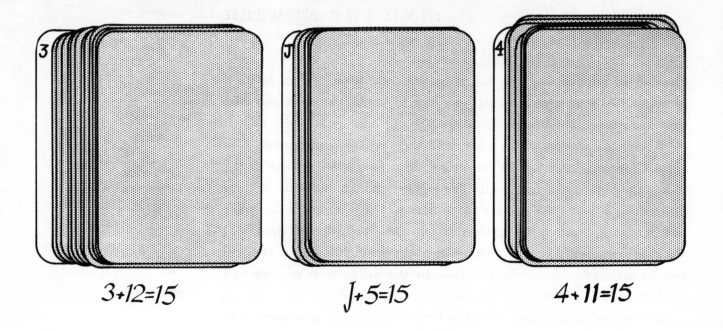

$3+12=15$ $J+5=15$ $4+11=15$

Figure 2

You begin to count silently on your fingers. Then you turn around and pick up the cards that are left over.

"I'll have this one. And this one. And this one."

Selecting two or three cards, you place them face down on the table.

You now ask your assistant to add up the values of his three face-up cards. Let us say that they were (for example) a two, a six, and a nine, thus totaling seventeen. You then turn over the cards that you yourself picked out. They, too, add up to seventeen!

How it is done

When you pick up the cards left over, you secretly count how many there are. Add *eight* to this number. The result will be the total value of the spectator's face-up cards.

In the example above, for instance, you would find nine cards left over. Adding eight would give you a total of seventeen. From the cards in your hand you would therefore pick out, say, a ten and a seven, or an eight, and a three, and a six.

If it happens that you can't find the right cards to add up to the number you want, you can bring in the aces, counting them each as one. Failing this, you would have to write the number on a piece of paper instead. But this difficulty will rarely, if ever, arise.

Points to remember

1. Make sure that your assistant knows how to count the face-down cards onto the face-up ones. The latter must be completely covered. You may find it wise to show him exactly what you mean, using the spare kings, queens, and aces, before you turn your back.

2. Note the subtle use of misdirection at the end of the trick. The fact that you are counting the leftover cards is well disguised by the perfectly natural action of picking them up to look for certain cards to add up to the number you want.

3. The counting on your fingers before you turn around is, of course, just bluff to mislead the spectators.

4. This trick can be performed again immediately if desired, and repetition may even enhance the effect. But don't overdo it. One repetition is enough.

THREE AND FOUR

The numbers three and four are particularly significant where cards are concerned. There are three court cards. There are four suits.

Here is a little experiment to show the power of these two numbers.

Begin by turning your back. Keep it turned throughout the trick. Ask a spectator to cut the pack into three heaps and to choose one of them. Then let him take his chosen heap and deal it into two smaller piles, giving one of them an *odd* number of cards and the other an *even* number. He need not deal every card in his hand.

Now (still with your back turned) remind your audience of the significance of the numbers three and four. Ask the spectator to multiply the number of cards in his *left*-hand pile by three, and the number in his *right*-hand pile by four. Then let him add the two results together and tell you what the final total is.

Putting your hand to your head you perform a quick calculation.

"The number of cards in your right-hand pile is odd, and the number in the left-hand pile is even."

This, of course, is an example. But whatever total he gives you, your instant calculation proves correct.

CARD TRICKS

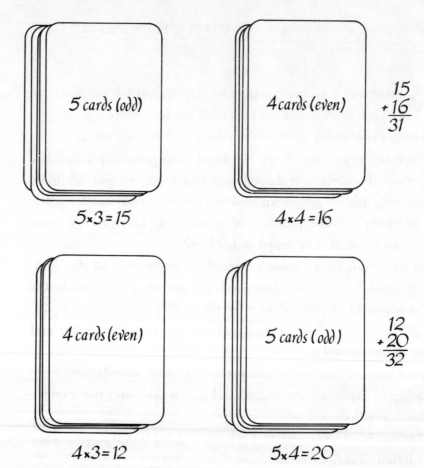

Figure 3

24

In spite of the hand you put to your head, as if making an elaborate calculation, this trick is very easy indeed. If the final total is an odd number, then the number of cards in the left-hand pile is odd too. If the total is an even number, the left-hand pile also has an even number of cards. Obviously the number of cards in the right-hand pile will be even when the left hand is odd, and odd when the left hand is even.

Do not perform the trick more than twice running, in case (unlikely though it may be) anyone notices that the left-hand result is always the same as the final total.

If you find it difficult to remember which heap is to be multiplied by three and which by four, note that L(eft) comes before R(ight), just as three comes before four.

Have you ever noticed that the diamonds are particularly sensitive cards?

You can demonstrate this in the following way. Go through the pack and pick out all the numbered diamonds, adding the joker to them. If there is no joker, use the jack of diamonds instead.

Lay these eleven cards face downward in a long row. A fair-sized table is desirable. If you haven't one available, then put the cards on the floor.

"When I turn my back," you may say, "will somebody move as many cards as he pleases, up to nine or ten, from the right-hand end of the row to the left-hand end? And please bear in mind three points. Firstly, move the cards one at a time. Secondly, don't pick them up but slide them over the table (or floor), keeping them face down. Thirdly, remember how many you move."

You move a couple of cards, one at a time, from the right of the row to the left, to show the chosen spectator how to do it. (It is a good plan to let the audience choose the spectator who is to move the cards.) Then you turn your back while he carries on with his task.

When he has moved the desired number of cards, he may, if he wants to, push all the cards along to the right, to make sure that you don't use a mark on the table to guess how many cards have been transferred.

As soon as he tells you he is ready, you turn to face the cards again. Without drawing special attention to it, you quietly remove a small magnet from your pocket and pass it slowly once or twice over the row of cards. Presently it seems to be drawn toward one particular card, and you let it come to rest on this card.

"How many cards did you move?" you ask.

Let us suppose that the answer is "five."

You turn up the card on which the magnet is lying. It is a five!

How it is done

The key to the mystery is the card which lies on the extreme right at the moment when you bring your magnet into play, for it indicates which card you must make the magnet choose. If the right-hand card is a three, for example, then the *third* card from the *left* will show how many cards have been moved. If the right-hand card is a four, then the *fourth* card from the left is the appropriate one.

The following lists should make the matter clear.

When you picked out the diamonds, you secretly **arranged them in** this order, counting from left to right:

List A

You moved two right-hand cards to the left to show the audience how to do it. That left the order as follows:

List B

The four is now the right-hand card, and when any cards are moved, the fourth card from the left will show how many. Suppose *three* cards are moved. Then the order will be:

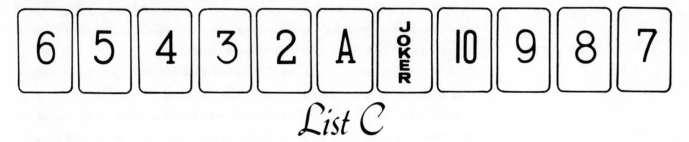

List C

As you will see, the fourth card is a three.

Try it for yourself with the cards set out in the order shown in *List B*, and you will find that the fourth card always shows the number of cards moved, however large or small that number may be.

This is a trick which bears repetition. Indeed, to do it again adds to the mystery, as the magnet this time will fall on a card in a different position. As a variation, you can turn up the card and *tell* the spectator how many cards he moved, instead of first asking him.

Remember that the right-hand card is no longer the four. But although the cards are face down, you can easily work out the number on the

Figure 4

right-hand one. Three cards were moved, so the right-hand card will be $4 + 3 = 7$. A glance at *List C* will show that this is so.

You will find that the *seventh* card from the left is now the one which indicates how many cards have been moved, so after letting your magnet roam backward and forward along the row of cards, make sure that in due course it comes to a halt at the seventh.

Do not lay a lot of stress on the use of this magnet, or your audience will begin to suspect that you are trying to bluff them. This, in fact, is exactly what you *are* trying to do, but the less fuss you make about it, the more effective your effort is likely to be. Just take the magnet quietly from your pocket as though it were the natural thing to do. At least some of your audience will probably be half-persuaded that magnetism somehow enters into the trick, even though they don't quite understand how.

If you have no magnet, you can use a comb, the smaller the better. Rub it briskly on your sleeve before using it, as though to bring out the magnetism, which a comb, in fact, often possesses.

Points to remember

1. Make sure that you have the eleven cards in the correct order before laying them face down in a row. It is a very simple order to remember.

2. Remember to move *two* cards, and only two, to show the audience how to do it, and remember, too, that this leaves the four at the right-hand end of the row.

3. If there is no joker, you will have to use the jack. But the joker can be useful if the audience try to trick you by moving no cards at all. In this event the magnet will fall on the joker, and the joke is on them when you turn it up.

4. The stress you lay on *sliding* the cards along the table, keeping them face down, is to discourage any inquisitive spectator from picking them up to see the order in which they are arranged.

"The king of hearts keeps wonderful discipline," you remark. "The cards in his suit always rush to obey the royal command. I'll show you what I mean."

Looking through the pack, you pick out the king of hearts and toss it face down on the table. Then, inviting a spectator to cut the pack into two halves, you pick up the half nearer to yourself and begin to run through it.

"Any heart will do. Here we are—here's the eight."

You put the card on top of your heap and ask the spectator to put the king on top of *his* heap.

"Now we bring them both to the middle."

You cut your cards, completing the cut, and invite him to do the same with his.

"Now your king is in the middle of *your* heap, and my eight is in the middle of *mine*. The problem is for the king to make the eight march across to join him. This is what we do to help the eight."

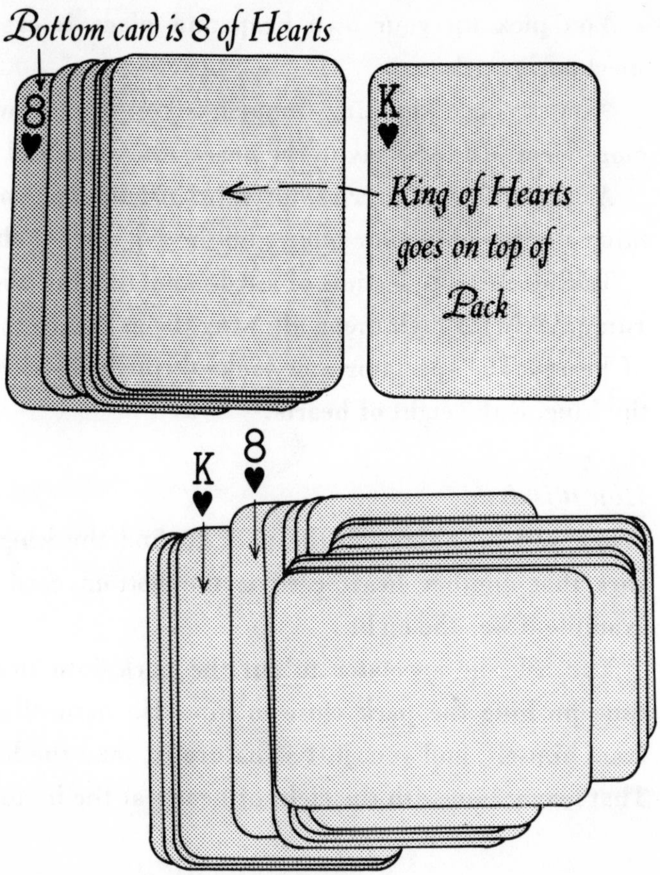

Bottom card is 8 of Hearts

*King of Hearts
goes on top of
Pack*

Figure 5

You pick up your own heap and place it crosswise on top of the spectator's cards.

"Try saying, 'The king commands you to appear, number eight!' The more vigorously you say it, the nearer the eight will come to the king."

As the spectator carries out your instruction, you help him by drumming a tattoo with your fingers on the top card of the pack.

Taking the top section of cards and turning them face upward, you run quickly through them, allowing the audience to see. There is no eight of hearts. The spectator now looks through his cards, and there, next to the king, is the eight of hearts!

How it is done

When you look through the pack to find the king of hearts, you make sure that another heart card is the bottom card of the pack. In our example it was the eight.

You ask the spectator to cut the pack into two halves, at the same time pushing the pack close to him. He naturally cuts the cards away from himself, and you, just as naturally, take the half nearer to yourself. That leaves him with the eight of hearts at the bottom of his half.

Looking through your cards for a heart, you pretend to have found the eight, though in fact the card you pick out is some other card. (It might as well be a heart.) You place it on top of your half, and then cut the cards, completing the cut. The spectator copies your action, thereby (unknown to himself) bringing the king and the eight together.

The trick is now over, apart from a little showmanship on your part.

Do not repeat this trick right away.

Look quickly through the cards to make sure that there is a joker in the pack. When you are satisfied that there is, you proceed to explain why you want him.

"The joker is quite useful in helping to find a chosen card. Choose one, and I'll show you how he does it."

You spread out the cards face down on the table, inviting a spectator to pick any card that takes his fancy and note what it is. While he is doing this, you gather up the cards so that he can drop his card on top of the pack. Cut the pack five times, spelling the word "j-o-k-e-r" as you do so—one letter for each completed cut.

"What happens is this," you continue. "The card which immediately follows the joker will nearly always reveal the position of a chosen card. For instance, if the joker is followed by a ten, then the chosen card will be the tenth card after that. A jack, by the way, counts eleven, a queen twelve, and a king thirteen."

You deal the cards face upward.

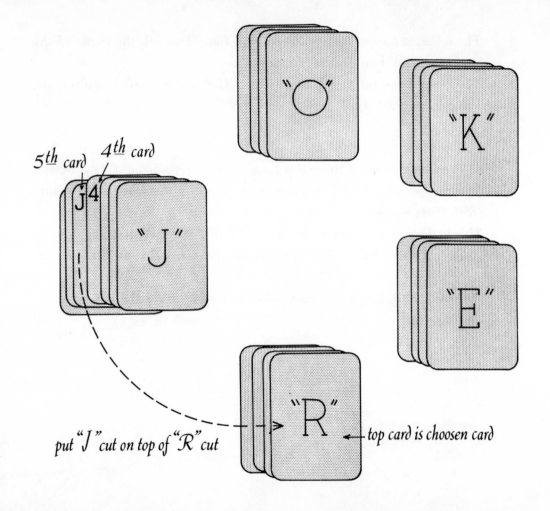

5<u>th</u> card 4<u>th</u> card

"O"

"K"

"J"

"E"

"R"

put "J" cut on top of "R" cut

top card is choosen card

Figure 6

The joker, it happens, is followed by a four. You ask the name of the chosen card, and then deal four more cards.

The joker lives up to his reputation. The fourth card is indeed the one that the spectator selected.

How it is done

When you look to see if there is a joker, you secretly bring a four of any suit to the position fourth from bottom, slipping the joker just behind it (fifth from bottom).

This is the whole secret of the trick. All that you now have to do is to talk convincingly of the joker's remarkable power, and then demonstrate it.

If there is no joker in the pack, you can decide to try the jack of clubs as a substitute.

Pick out the spades, from the queen down to the ace, discarding only the king. Then set out the twelve cards face downward in the form of a rather unusual clock, as shown in Figure 7. Each hour on the dial is represented by a single face-down card, although the numbers are not in the customary position.

The spades, you explain, are the best educated of the four suits, and are particularly good at figures. You have therefore chosen them to help you with this trick.

Ask someone to think of any hour he pleases on a twelve-hour clock— in other words, a number from one to twelve. Tell him to write it down on a piece of paper, so that there can be no mistake afterward, but warn him to take care, at this stage, that nobody else knows what hour he has written.

"The spades have their own clock system," you explain. "They're also thought readers. It doesn't matter what time you want to be called. They seem to know just when it is without being told."

39

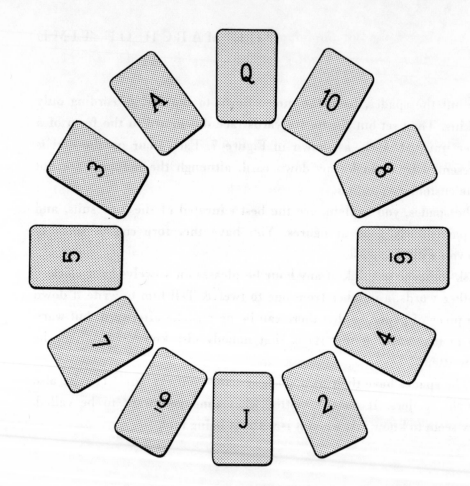

Figure 7

"I'm going to tap out the hours in haphazard order, to indicate the passing of time. Will you *silently* count as I tap, beginning on the hour that you chose. Go on counting with each tap until twenty is reached. At this point—that is, on the number 20—call '*Stop.*' "

Let us suppose that the spectator mentally chose six o'clock as his hour. He should mentally count "six" on your first tap, "seven" on your second tap, and so on until he comes to "twenty," when he calls "Stop."

You now turn up the card on which your pencil came to rest. It is the six—the very number which the spectator mentally chose.

No matter what hour is chosen, if the spectator does his counting correctly, your pencil is always found to have stopped at the spade which indicates that number. The spades have read his thoughts!

How it is done

The spades should be picked out in the following order:

Q, 10, 8, 6, 4, 2, J, 9, 7, 5, 3, A

That is, the queen followed by the even cards in descending order, and the jack followed by the odd cards in descending order. The queen, of course, stands for twelve, the jack for eleven.

41

Lay them face downward in the form of a clock, starting with the queen at the top and going around in a clockwise direction.

Your first eight taps may fall on any cards you please, on either side of the clock. Your *ninth* tap, however, must be on the queen at the top, your tenth on the jack at the bottom, your eleventh on the ten, and then on the nine, eight, seven, six, in this reverse order, down to the ace.

If you do your tapping in this way, then, when the number 20 is reached, your pencil will automatically be resting on the chosen number.

Do not be in too much of a hurry with your tapping. Give the pencil time to rest firmly, for a second or two, on each card it touches.

Points to remember

1. You can perform the trick once or twice more if you wish, without giving away the secret.

2. The unusual clock arrangement is easy enough to remember once you have got the hang of it. But just to start with, if you find any difficulty, practice it a few times with the cards face up.

3. If desired, the cards can be laid out face upward with the cards in the same order as the figures on an ordinary clock dial. This, in fact, is the conventional way of performing the trick. But it has the disadvantage

that the spectator who chose the hour can soon see in advance that the pencil will stop on his number. There is thus no element of surprise in the finish of the trick. With the cards set out as in Figure 7, no one really knows which card you are going to tap next, or what the numbers are on the cards you are tapping, and interest is thus maintained for the climax.

This is a good trick with which to follow "The March of Time." You pick up the cards already on the table and add the king to them.

"The spades," you remark, "are not only good at figures. They're also quite clever at spelling—perhaps because *spa*des and *spe*lling begin with the same letters."

With the packet of spades in your hands, you offer to show what you mean.

"A . . . C . . . E spells *ace,*" you say. Each time you mention a letter you move a card from the top to the bottom of the packet in your hands. Three cards have thus been transferred. You place the fourth face up on the table—and it is none other than the ace.

You leave it on the table and spell the next number, transferring cards as before.

"T . . . W . . . O spells *two.*"

Again you turn up the next card and place it on the table. It is the two.

Steadily you go through the numbers in turn, moving a card from top to bottom each time you say a letter. After the last letter of every card, you put the next card face upward on the table. Each time it turns out to be the card whose name you have just spelled. When you have spelled the ten, you go on to the jack in just the same way, and with the same result.

By the time the queen is reached, you have only two cards left in your hands. But you continue to change them over as you spell Q . . . U . . . E . . . E . . . N. The card you turn over is indeed the queen, and only the king is left.

How it is done

The trick looks like a piece of very clever sleight of hand, but it is in fact simplicity itself. The whole secret lies in the arrangement of the cards. If you gather them up correctly, then the trick performs itself.

The order of the cards from top to bottom, with the cards face down, is as follows:

3, 8, 7, A, Q, 6, 4, 2, J, K, 10, 9, 5

You may find it easier to remember this order if you split the numbers up into five little groups.

3   8   7

ace queen

6   4   2

jack   king

10   9   5

Figure 8

Recite this several times to yourself, and you will soon know it by heart.

1. This trick follows the previous one very neatly. You know the arrangements of the cards in "The March of Time," although the cards are face down. It is easy to gather them up in the correct order for the spelling trick, and your audience will not have the least idea that you are doing so. Pick up the three first, place the eight beneath it, the seven beneath that, and so on. Finally you take the king from the pack, slip it casually between the jack and the ten, and you are ready to show the spectators how well the spades can spell.

2. If you want to perform the trick without preceding it with "The March of Time," you will have to begin by running through the cards face upward, putting the spades, as you come to them, in the correct order on the face of the pack. If you make this the first trick in your performance, the spades can already be in the desired order.

Deal the cards into three heaps, each containing sixteen cards, and ask a spectator to choose two of the heaps. As you push the discarded heap aside, you say to him, "Take one of the two heaps you've chosen, turn the cards face up, and make a mental note of *one* of them. Remember what it is, and also remember its position from the bottom—that is to say, counting from the right when the cards are face up."

As an example, we will suppose that the spectator mentally chooses the three of diamonds, the twelfth card from the bottom. (Fig. 9.)

Turning to another spectator, you ask him to whisper in your ear a number between twenty and thirty. We will suppose that he whispers the number 22.

"Obviously I can't possibly know the card you thought of," you say to the first spectator. "But I'm going to make a magical guess and try to put your card in the position chosen by our friend."

Gathering the two heaps into one, you consult the top card, move a few cards from the top to the bottom, and finally riffle the cards.

"I think that should do it," you remark.

12th. card from bottom

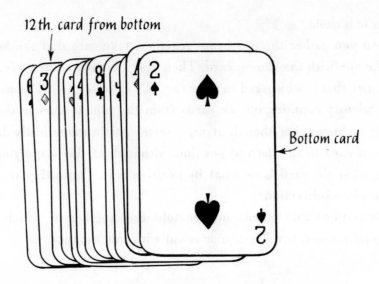

Bottom card

Now for the first time you ask what the chosen card was, and its position.

"It was the three of diamonds and it was number twelve," you are told.

"Our friend wanted it to appear at number twenty-two. Let's see if it does."

Starting at twelve, you count to twenty-two. And, sure enough, card number 22 is the three of diamonds.

Figure 9

How it is done

When you gather the two heaps together, take care that the lower heap is the one with the chosen card. Then you mentally subtract from 32 the number that is whispered in your ear. In our example, 22 from 32 leaves 10. Silently counting off ten cards from the top, you move them to the bottom. Surprising though it may seem, this automatically brings the chosen card to the desired position, although at this stage you have no idea what the card is or what its position was. Consulting the top card is simply misdirection.

Remember that when you are told the number at which the card originally stood, you begin your count with *that number*.

I'M ALWAYS RIGHT!

To perform this trick, you first go through the pack, picking out a few cards which you place on the table in two small heaps. Taking two folded slips of paper from your pockets, you hold them in your hands for a few moments, as if deliberating. Then you replace one of them in your pocket and pass the other to a spectator.

"Place this on either of the two heaps," you request. The note states definitely which heap you are going to choose. "I never make a mistake in this experiment. My prediction is *always* right."

When the spectator, after as much hesitation as he pleases, at length places the note on one of the heaps, you ask him to open and read it.

"You will place this note on the *five* heap," the message states.

You pick up the chosen heap, slowly count the cards in it, and reveal that he has selected a heap containing five cards. The other heap, as you proceed to show, contains only four cards.

And if anyone is wondering what the other note said, you promptly reveal this too. Removing it from your pocket, you read the message aloud.

"You will place this note on the *four* heap," it states.

Somehow, it seems, you knew without any question that he was going to choose the *five* heap and not the *four* heap. But how?

How it is done

The cards you pick out are the four fives and five of the court cards. The fives go into one heap, the court cards into the other. If you get into the habit of putting the fives always on the left and the court cards on the right, you will not forget which heap is which.

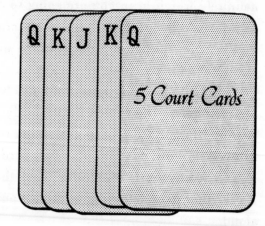

Figure 10

In your left-hand jacket pocket (assuming you're a boy) you have a carefully folded note which states: "You will place this note on the *five* heap." This is the note which you hand to a spectator.

In your right-hand pocket you have two more folded notes. One says: "You will place this note on the *four* heap." The other says: "You will place this note on the *court card* heap." The notes are kept apart by, say, a wallet.

It does not matter on which heap the spectator places the message.

(*a*) If he puts it on the right-hand heap, you count the five cards slowly *face down*, pointing out that he has chosen the heap containing five cards, not the heap of four cards.

"If you had chosen this *four* heap, I would have given you the other note," you boldly inform the spectator, drawing from your right-hand pocket the appropriate message.

(*b*) On the other hand, if he had placed the note on the left-hand heap, you would have turned the cards *face up*, revealing that they were all fives, whereas the cards in the other heap were all court cards. And you would be ready to show that the right-hand pocket contained a note stating that the court cards would be chosen.

What could be fairer than that?

Points to remember

1. You must not forget which note is which in your right-hand pocket. To avoid mistakes, always keep the court card note on the outside (that is, to the right of the wallet).

2. You cannot repeat this trick without danger of disclosing the secret. If you are asked to do so, you may explain that your power of prediction grows weaker after the first infallible guess. Then do another prediction trick instead, such as "Odd or Even," the next trick in this book.

Ask a spectator to cut the pack into four or five heaps and to choose one of them.

"Just count the number of cards it contains, to see whether the number is odd or even."

While he is doing this, you gather up the rest of the cards and deal out two small heaps.

"Choose whichever one you please," you say, "and add the cards to those you already hold. And I predict that no matter which heap you choose, or how many cards you have, the number will be altered from odd to even, or from even to odd."

He makes his choice and adds the two heaps together. And when he counts up, he finds that your prediction was correct. If his heap was originally even, it has now become odd; if it was originally odd, it has now become even.

How it is done

The two heaps you offer him are both odd, containing, say, nine cards and eleven cards, respectively. To add an odd number to an even num-

55

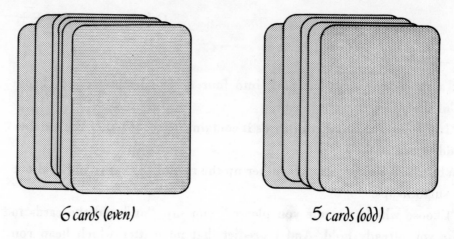

6 cards (even)   5 cards (odd)

Your heaps contain 9 and 11 cards, respectively (both odd). Thus:

6+9=15

5+11=16

But if both your heaps are even, such as 8 and 10, the result is:

6+8=14

5+10=15

Figure 11

56

ber makes it odd. To add an odd number to an odd number makes it even. Your prediction, therefore, cannot fail to be right.

To show that you can alter your prediction at will, you may perform the trick again, but this time predicting that there will be no change. That is to say, if the spectator's heap is odd, it will remain odd, and if it is even, it will remain even.

To achieve this, you merely have to deal two *even* heaps for him to choose from, and your prediction will again be right.

"This is a little test to see if you have magic fingers," you tell a spectator. "Deal yourself ten cards. Then fan them out with the faces toward you, while I turn my back. Choose one of them, and note what number it stands at, counting from the right."

You take the cards from him, put them behind your back for a few moments, and riffle them.

"Although I can't possibly know what your card is, I've carried out a secret move to help you. Now you must carry out a magical move yourself. But we'll make yours an easy one. What was the number your card stood at, counting from the right?"

Let us suppose the spectator gives four as the number. You return the cards to him face down.

"Just move four cards from the bottom to the top, one at a time."

When he has done that, ask him to hand you the top card.

"Keep the next one for yourself by putting it underneath the other cards. That's right. Give the next one to me. Thanks. Keep the next for yourself by putting it at the bottom."

Under your guidance he continues the process, alternately giving you a card and putting one at the bottom, until at last there is only one card left.

He names his chosen card, and then turns over the card in his hand. It is the very same card!

"You certainly have magic fingers," you tell him kindly.

Figure 12

How it is done

When you put the cards behind your back, you do, as you say, carry out a secret move. With the cards held face down, you transfer three cards from the bottom to the top. The trick then works itself.

The court cards, you point out, are different from the other cards because every king, queen, and jack has a mouth and is therefore able to speak.

You proceed to demonstrate the truth of this by removing all the court cards and shuffling them. Spreading them face down in a wide fan, you ask a spectator to slide one out upon the table.

When he has done this, ask him to take a careful look at it, making sure that you do not see the face of it. Then get him to slide it back into the fan, anywhere he pleases, and to shuffle the cards.

Placing them in a face-up packet on the table, you take up one card at a time and place it to your ear.

"He [or she] says 'No,' " you comment, putting the card down.

The same thing happens with almost every card. But one of them has a different message for your ear.

"He [or she] says 'Yes,' " you observe, holding up the card. "This is the card you chose."

And the spectator confirms that you are correct.

How it is done

On the court cards in many packs you will find that the margin on one side of the picture is slightly wider than the margin on the other side. Before you begin your performance, arrange the twelve cards so that the wider margins are all on the right-hand side.

Hold the cards in the form of a face-down fan in your right hand for the spectator to choose his card. While he is carefully looking at it, close the fan with your left hand and hold the cards with your left fingers at one end and your right fingers at the other end. Reopen the fan, keeping the cards in the left hand. They will now be reversed, so that when the spectator returns his card, it will be in a position opposite to the rest. The wider margin will be on the left-hand side instead of the right-hand side.

Before lifting each card to put it to your ear, you must glance quickly at the margins. When you lift the card with its margins reversed, you pretend that this one has whispered "Yes."

Do not let the audience see you looking hard at the cards. Try to imagine that you are *really* listening.

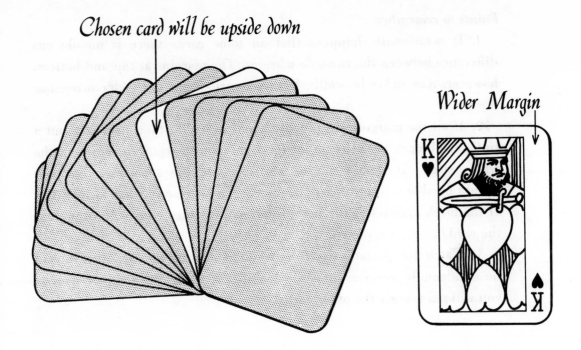

Chosen card will be upside down

Wider Margin

Figure 13

Points to remember

1. It occasionally happens that on some cards there is no obvious difference between the two side margins. The margins at top and bottom, however, may differ in width. If they do, then put the wider margin at the top.

2. If all the margins are roughly equal in width, then privately put a tiny pencil mark near the top of the right-hand margin, to represent the wide margin. It should not be noticeable to the spectators, but you should be able to spot it easily since you know exactly what to look for. If the mark appears at the bottom left-hand corner, you will know that the card has been reversed.

3. Watch the spectator carefully when he chooses his card, just in case he accidentally reverses it while looking at it. If he does, of course, you will not reverse the other cards.

Pick out the eight of clubs, nine of spades, eight of hearts, and nine of diamonds, and put them face down on the table. Then cut the pack into three roughly equal heaps.

Show the four cards by dealing them face upward on the table, saying as you do, "Club, spade, heart, diamond.

"Although they belong to different suits," you remark, gathering them up, "these four cards, the eights and the nines, are firm friends. They can't bear to be separated. Let me show you what I mean."

Insert two of the cards at different positions in one of the three heaps. Then insert the remaining two cards in another of the heaps. Put the two heaps together and shuffle them thoroughly. Place them on the third heap and cut the cards once.

Tap the pack four times with the knuckle of your forefinger.

"That's the signal to bring them together. As soon as they hear that, all four cards do their very best to gather for a meeting in the middle of the pack. And here they are—club, spade, heart, diamond."

Run through the cards face upward. There, in a group together in the middle, are The Four Friends.

Group 1

Figure 14

Group 2

It is not easy for the audience to remember clearly two rather similar cards. It is even more difficult to remember two *pairs* of similar cards. The cards you show first are eight of clubs, nine of spades, eight of hearts, nine of diamonds. (Let us call them Group 1.) But the cards which, at the end of the trick, appear together in the middle of the pack are nine of clubs, eight of spades, nine of hearts, eight of diamonds. (Let us call these Group 2.) It will be a very astute spectator who notices the difference.

Begin by picking out Group 1 and placing them face down on the table. While doing so, you also secretly pick out Group 2, placing these cards at the bottom of the pack. Then cut the pack into three heaps, A, B, and C, heap A being the one with Group 2 cards at the bottom.

Pick up the four cards in Group 1 from the table and show them, giving the audience just enough time to see that they are black and red eights and nines, but not enough time to make a careful note of each individual card. Insert two of them in heap B, two in heap C. When the three heaps are put together, see that heap A is at the bottom.

One completed cut will now bring Group 2 to the middle of the pack, and in due course you reveal them as The Four Friends.

Remove the court cards and the tens from the pack. Shuffle the remaining cards, and then spread them face down along the table. Ask a spectator to choose one, and offer him a pencil and a piece of paper.

"Whatever the number is on your card, double it. Have you done that? Then add five. Have you done that? Then multiply by five."

Invite another spectator to choose a card. Get him to add the number on that card to the total worked out by the first spectator, and to write down the result on a separate slip of paper and pass it to you.

As soon as you have examined this, you pick up a section of the cards on the table and hold them in a fan facing you. From this fan of cards (or possibly from a second or third fan) you select two cards.

The spectators' cards are now turned face up. Immediately you reveal your own two cards. They bear just the same values as the spectators' cards.

How it is done

When you select your cards, you obviously pick out two which (ignoring

5- *double it = 10*
add 5 = 15
multiply by 5 = 75

75+8=83
83-25=58

The two numbers are respectively 5 and 8.

Figure 15

suits) are identical with the cards chosen by the spectators. But how do you know what the spectators' cards are?

The answer is surprisingly simple. You merely subtract 25 from the total given to you. This will leave you with a two-figure answer, and the two figures will always represent the numbers on the spectators' cards.

Let us take an example.

The first spectator draws a five.

Points to remember

1. Do the subtraction sum in your head if you can. (You may find it easiest to subtract 5 first and then 20.) But if you have to work it out on paper, don't leave the paper lying about where it may expose your method of doing the trick. Put it in your pocket, and destroy it later.

2. If you wish, instead of removing the court cards and tens, you can tell the spectators to disregard these cards, if they happen to select one, and to have another choice.

3. To help you remember the order in which the calculations should be carried out, think of the word "dam."

Shuffle the cards and ask a spectator to cut the pack into two halves, more or less equal in size. Pushing the top half aside (it is not used in the trick), invite him to cut the lower half again into two roughly equal heaps. Hand him the upper of these two heaps, inviting him first to shuffle it and then to look at the two top cards.

Offer him a piece of paper and a pencil.

"Write down what the cards are, so that there won't be any mistake. But take care not to let me see them or see what you write."

When he has done this and then replaced the two top cards, put the two heaps together. Ask him to cut the cards two or three times, completing the cut each time.

Take the cards yourself and lay them down face upward in four or five rows.

You now produce your patent Lie Detector, which may be just a piece of electric cord or other wire. Direct your victim to hold one end in his left hand and use his other hand to hold the paper on which he has written the names of his cards. The opposite end of the wire is held in your own left hand.

"I'm going to touch various cards," you tell him. "Each time I touch a card I shall ask you if it's one of those you chose. You can answer Yes or No just as you please, without regard to the truth. But if my Lie Detector is working properly, I'll know whenever you tell me a lie. I get a kind of faint electric shock."

And unless something goes wrong, your verdict is right every time.

How it is done

When you first shuffle the cards, give a quick glance at the bottom card, taking care not to stare at it. Let us suppose it is the three of spades. After the spectator has written down the names of his cards, you bring the two heaps together by dropping the lower heap on the upper heap. This brings the three of spades immediately above the two chosen cards. (Fig. 16.)

As you lay the cards down in rows you must watch for the three of spades. The two cards which immediately follow it will be the chosen ones.

Since you now know the identity of these cards you can easily detect whether your victim is lying when he answers Yes or No to your query. But don't be in too much of a hurry in delivering your verdict. Try to imagine that you really receive an electric shock whenever a lie is told.

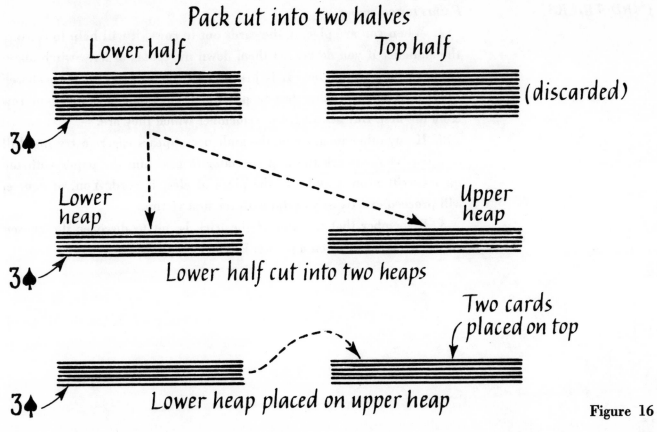

Pack cut into two halves

Lower half   Top half

(discarded)

3♠

Lower heap   Upper heap

3♠

Lower half cut into two heaps

Two cards placed on top

3♠   Lower heap placed on upper heap

Figure 16

73

Points to remember

1. When you are placing the cards out in rows, it will help to confuse the audience if you do not set them down in regular order. Switch about from one row to another. It is just as well not to place the two chosen cards next to each other but to put the second one in a different row from the first. But be careful to remember which they are.

2. If any other member of the audience appears eager to try his skill as a liar, you may ask the first spectator to pass him the paper with the names written on it and also the piece of electric cord. You, of course, will proceed exactly as you did with the first victim.

3. Remember that the aim of the trick is not to discover the chosen cards but to detect when a person is lying.

If you perform a trick a second time, it is a good idea to use quite a different method, to confuse the audience. Here is another way of detecting lies.

Begin by getting a spectator to place ten cards face downward and to put his finger on one of them. Without looking at its face yourself, hold it up so that the whole audience can see its identity.

Replace it, and then ask the spectator to gather up the cards, mix them together in any way he pleases, and hand them to you.

"Now I'm going to show them to you one at a time," you tell him. "I want you each time to say, 'That's my card' or 'That's not my card,' without regard to the truth. I can't see what the cards are, but I think I'll be able to detect when you're lying by the tone of your voice."

You hold up each card with its back toward you. If you like, you can have your eyes bandaged while you do this. It makes no difference. You are able without fail to tell when your victim is lying.

How it is done

When you hold up the card for the audience to note its identity, your right thumbnail makes a small dent in the corner of the card. As you pass the card to the other hand to show it to those on your left, your left thumbnail makes a similar dent in the opposite corner. (Fig. 17.)

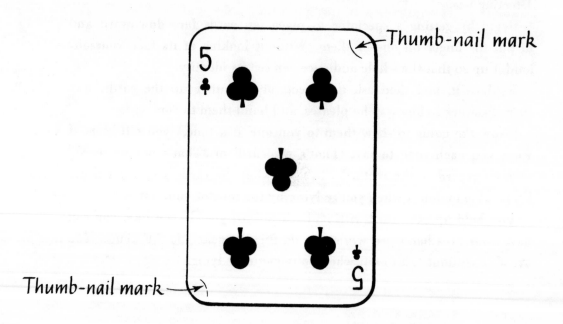

Figure 17

Even if your eyes are bandaged, you can easily feel the tiny bump as you take the card in your fingers to show it to your victim. Thus you know at once when you are holding the chosen card and whether he is lying or not in his replies.

You must take care not to be seen feeling for the bump. Pretend to be giving all your attention to the spectator's voice, and occasionally get him to repeat his answer.

Seven is a very important number. There are seven days in the week, Seven Wonders of the World, seven ages in man's life. The seventh son of a seventh son is supposed to be an exceptional person.

Ask a spectator to deal seven cards face down and to take a peep at one of them. He must remember its identity, but he must not let you see its face.

Taking out a long pencil, you tap the back of the chosen card seven times.

"Now I know the sound of it," you say.

Ask him to collect the seven cards and cut them two or three times, so that you cannot tell which is the chosen one. Then let him deal them out again in a row, this time face upward.

You go along the row, tapping each card in turn with your pencil. Possibly you do this more than once. But at last you come to a decision.

"*That's* your card." You give one of them an extra tap.

The spectator admits that you are perfectly right, and that you have picked out, apparently by the sound, the very card that he looked at.

As you collect the cards from a previous trick, make a mental note of the card which goes on top of the pack. (Suppose it is the six of diamonds, for instance.)

Apparently mix up the cards by cutting them into five or six heaps and then gathering the heaps up in random order. Actually take care that the heap with the six of diamonds on top becomes the top heap.

The spectator deals out the top seven cards, naturally putting the top card (six of diamonds) at the extreme left of the row.

Let us suppose that the cards he puts down are as follows, though face downward:

Let us suppose, too, that he peeps at the nine of spades, the fourth card from the six. Make a mental note of its position.

Watch carefully as he collects the cards. If he does this by putting the six on the jack, the two together on the four, and so on along the row, then, when the cards are laid out again face upward, the chosen card will still be the fourth card *after* the six. For example:

On the other hand, if he collects the cards by putting the two on the seven, the seven on the nine of spades, and so on along the row, then the chosen card will be the fourth card *before* the six. For example:

You can collect and cut the cards yourself if you prefer to do so, but it is better to let the spectator do it if you feel confident enough to let him.

Note that the above examples should make clear the method of counting. If you are counting forward (that is, to the right) and come to the end of the row before finishing the count, continue from the left-hand end. If you are counting backward (that is, to the left), continue from the right-hand end.

Figure 18

"I'm told that the clubs are heavier than other cards," you remark. "Let's see if it's true."

A spectator shuffles the cards and then deals a little packet of six face down on the table. Without looking at them, he places them in your hands behind your back.

You feel them carefully, and then say that two of them seem heavier than the rest. Bringing your hands forward, you find that there are indeed two clubs, and that the remaining four are diamonds, hearts, or spades.

The audience may examine the clubs as much as they like, but they will find nothing suspicious. It appears that your sensitive fingers alone are responsible for the trick.

How it is done
To perform this trick you need a second pack similar to the one you are going to use for your other tricks. From it you take six cards, of which two must be clubs. Before beginning your performance you slip this little packet in your hip pocket, with two clubs on top.

When you are supposed to be feeling the cards for weight, you are in fact exchanging the six cards in your hands for the six in your pocket. You must practice this exchange in front of a mirror until you can do it quite smoothly.

Before bringing the cards forward, take the two clubs in your right hand, leaving the other four cards in your left.

You will need to exchange the two packets once more before the cards can be freely used, so this had better be one of the last tricks in your performance.

two clubs on top

Figure 19

82

You introduce this trick by narrating a little story.

"There was once a wealthy European merchant who retired to a remote country village with his three sons. When the sons grew up, they all decided to go off and seek their fortunes, and their father agreed to help them, each according to his age. To the eldest son he gave $3,000, to the middle son $2,000, and to the youngest son $1,000."

You ask if three members of the audience will kindly represent the sons. Then, taking a pack of cards, you select the red cards (hearts and diamonds), which, you explain, are particularly suitable for fortune-telling. To the person representing the eldest son, you give *three* cards, to the middle son, *two* cards, and to the youngest son, *one* card.

"They all went their different ways. One went into the army. Another became a successful engineer. The third went overseas."

You produce three slips of paper bearing, respectively, the words "army," "engineer," and "overseas."

"The one who went into the army had a steady job, but he didn't make a great deal of money. The engineer did rather better for himself.

As for the one who went overseas, he managed to make a small fortune in the oil business."

You turn to the three people representing the sons and invite them, when you go out of the room, to decide among themselves which career they would like to adopt, and to take and conceal the slip of paper bearing the appropriate name. When they have made their decisions, the army man should take the *same number* of cards (from the red suits) as he already holds, the engineer *twice as many* as he already holds, and the man who went overseas *four times as many* as he already holds.

You bring forward a sheet of paper on which these details are written, just in case there is any doubt. (Fig. 20.) Then you leave the room while the decisions are made and the necessary cards taken. When you return, you continue the story.

Figure 20

ARMY :   Same number as he holds
ENGINEER : Twice as many as he holds
OVERSEAS : Four times as many as he holds

"Years passed, and the father failed to hear from his sons how they were faring. At last he became anxious to know just what had happened, and he called in a fortune-teller."

You pick up the hearts and diamonds that have been left over after the three "sons" have taken the requisite cards, and arrange them in any way that you please, carefully examining the face of each card.

"After consulting some red playing cards, the fortune-teller announced that the youngest son had gone overseas, the middle son was an engineer, and the eldest son an officer in the army." (These, of course, are merely examples.)

As you make each prediction, you turn to the "son" concerned and invite him to show the slip of paper he holds. All three predictions are shown to be right.

How it is done
There is strong misdirection in this very mysterious trick. Your careful study of the cards is just to deceive the audience. What you really do is to count the number of cards left over. This number, in a rather subtle way, will reveal to you which person holds each slip of paper.

85

The knowledge is gained by means of a secret formula, consisting of six words easily learned by heart: *Are Beans Carbon? Eton Forward Goes.*

1. A r E   A E (O)
2. b E A n s   E A (O)
3. c A rb O n   A O (E)
4.
5. E t O n   E O (A)
6. f O rw A rd   O A (E)
7. g O E s   O E (A)

Notice the following points:

(*a*) The numbers refer to the number of cards left over.

(*b*) Each of the six words contains *two* of the letters A, E, or O in a certain order.

(*c*) A stands for Army, E for Engineer, O for Overseas.

(*d*) In each case the order of persons is youngest, middle, eldest. The letter for the eldest is given in parentheses; it is obvious that it must always be the letter left over after the first two letters have been revealed.

(*e*) The six words are in alphabetical order, with D omitted. The omission is because it never happens that just *four* cards are left over.

Let us take an example.

Suppose you find *five* cards left over. The fifth letter in the alphabet is E, so it is easy enough to remember that the appropriate word is *Eton*. The order of letters is therefore E O. That means that the youngest son is the engineer, and the middle son went overseas. The eldest, therefore, must obviously have gone into the army.

All that remains for you to do is to pretend to study the faces of the five leftover cards, and in due course to announce the information that they have secretly given you.

Points to remember

1. Pay great attention (without overexaggeration) to the faces of the leftover cards, because these have nothing to do with the trick!

2. The reason for selecting only the red cards is just to mislead the audience. The important thing is to have exactly twenty-four cards, but in order to avoid conveying to the audience that numbers enter into the matter, you pretend to be concerned only with the suits. You do not, in fact, take *all* the red cards. As there are twenty-six red cards, you take

care to leave two of them behind; but you do not, of course, mention this. It is a good plan to leave the aces. Then if anyone notices that two red cards are left, you can explain that the aces, having neither a picture nor a number, are not very good for fortune-telling.